TIME OUT TIME

Dagger Editions, an imprint of Caitlin Press Inc.
3375 Ponderosa Way
Qualicum Beach, BC V9K 2J8
www.daggereditions.com/www.caitlin-press.com

Text and cover design by Vici Johnstone
Cover art by Diana Smith
Printed in Canada

Caitlin Press Inc. acknowledges financial support from the Government of Can-
ada and the Canada Council for the Arts, and the Province of British Columbia
through the British Columbia Arts Council and the Book Publisher's Tax Credit.

Library and Archives Canada Cataloguing in Publication

Time out of time : poems / Arleen Paré.
Paré, Arleen, author.

Canadiana 20210314893 | ISBN 9781773860794 (softcover)

LCC PS8631.A7425 T56 2022 | DDC C811/.6—dc23

TIME OUT OF TIME

poems

ARLEEN PARÉ

DAGGER EDITIONS, 2022

"In her seventh decade, Paré encounters Etel Adnan's *Time*. As she reads it, she hears 'the hush/the pages make.' Inspired, she gives herself over to Adnan's sheer attentiveness of 'writing backwards,' and chronology, fixed meaning, syntax, and privacy—reconfigure and vivify her recollections and musings. Alert: you will read this book more than once!"

—Betsy Warland, author of
Bloodroot—Tracing the Untelling of Motherloss, 2nd edition, 2021

"Graceful, sensual, and evocative, Arleen Paré's latest collection pays fitting homage to the poetry of the late Etel Adnan. *Time Out of Time* is also very much its own text, moving and beguiling, and expanding in multiple directions as it explores mortality, lesbian identity, and queer poetics."

—Annick MacAskill, author of
Swimming Upwards and *Murmurations*

In praise and celebration of poet Etel Adnan.

Note from the Author

In April, my poet friend Maureen Hynes suggested I read *Time* by Etel Adnan. It was love at first page. The poems in *Time* are spare and exquisitely structured. And then I discovered the remarkable Etel Adnan herself! Born in 1925 in Beirut, the daughter of a Greek Christian mother and a Syrian Muslim father, she studied in France and spoke several languages. While protesting France's war in Algeria, Adnan stopped writing in French, which meant she stopped writing poetry altogether for that period of time. Instead, she began painting. Not only was she an internationally recognized poet and painter, she was also a novelist, a philosopher, a polyglot, a public intellectual and a teacher. She won the Lambda Award for Lesbian Poetry, the California Book Award, and France's l'Ordre de Chevalier des Arts et des Lettres, among others. In her lifetime she wrote over a dozen books in English, and other languages. In 2020, *Time* won the Griffin Poetry Prize. Fully smitten, I have employed the poetics in *Time* to shape this tribute collection.

On the morning of November 14, 2021, before this book went to print, Etel Adnan died in Paris, the city of light. She was ninety-six. I was broken-hearted; I thought she would live forever.

The volume of narrative,
its wide-reaching, long-lasting
exponentiates to boredom

it's funny sometimes
strange
sometimes a bit blurry

right now I have only words on my mind
no story at all
no plotline, tangents, or around and she said, she said

soft-hearted showers pulled the boards, the streets
and on its merge, worked

is now in something else
a bucket of memory
a bowl of clear water
a couple bright, beating words
three or four unresolved thoughts

When you realize you are mortal, you also realize the tremendousness of the future.
—Etel Adnan

Etel Adnan 1

the first *Time* is
in an empty bank 2 p.m.
first page
masked
the Pandemic
empties out all ambient noise
the hush
the pages make as they turn
untiming
the glass doors monumental
onto the unpeopled street

2

I want to follow you
into your small
verbal squares
elegant   spare
enough cut
enough cut

follow you there   despite
claustrophobia   those five fearsome syllables
the o tight in the middle
3 p.m.   even the word wants release
nonetheless
nonetheless

3

I would follow you anywhere
leave the pear halved
on the plate
meet you at O'Hare or Heathrow or at Marrakesh Menara
get lost once again
or forever
in your words
just your words
with or without any meaning
the shape of them
in perfect translation
I don't even know
what you look like

4

would I pursue her if
she didn't play on the same team   if
I knew
what she looked like
would I trail her into tentative
darkness   follow her
on a voyage of no return
track her to the edge of evil and good
stanza after sweet-smelling stanza
with no punctuation

no question
no question mark

5

when she entrusts us to what's subterrain
will we find
what's buried beneath
beetles   broken glass   rats
root systems   teeth

when she says happiness is unbearable on page 67
despite how much
we love her
does it deflect us from peace

she   a small moveable organism
bespeaking hope
even when hope is in hiding

6

I now know what you look like
on Google
you smile
you are seated
you speak English Arabic French and
you write in all three
you paint
small squares of colour
you are now ninety-six
I know you best
in your small squares of mentation

7

This heat   relentless mid-day
the boiling point
in measures of Kelvin
a scale wherein
zero
reflects total absence

starting in Glasgow
as did my father

time
its arrow depending
on heat
for its forward direction

what I watch is the cinders   entropic
ash with blurring black wings

8

Time is how we measure change.

—unknown

if you are lucky
in time
you will never stop
smiling

death is a collective perception
an unwavering bond
a staunch transformation
it will arrive

if you are lucky
you will die full of days

is there anything that does not
lead in this dreamy direction

9

although I respect its provenance
its friendly corresponding intent
I cannot
call your poems *postcard poems*
as if
they were tossed off at poolside
somewhere club med   *blue sky*
wish you were here

do your lines handhold such modest heft

as if Sappho's fragments
can be forgotten

does brevity not bear
its fair share
of depth

Mother of Lyric

When Sappho came down from the high meadows wreathed in butterflies
white and soft yellow   with two maidens   one at each side   which is what she
preferred   each wearing lavender wrapped round their wrists and their waists
all expectation though they knew only to write with a stylus   not to bounce babies
or to boil broth   only to hold up their hands   all praise and forbearance
only to scratch words   flowers and flight   words that meant love
which was what she preferred

As opposed to Homeric   though in truth Sappho would not have used the word
oppose   in her sapphist/bi/queer/lyric/lavender lifestyle   in her encounters she
would not have used the word *enantionomai*   even in fragments   how could a
fragment oppose   how could the lyric   even when sundered its edges do not
become teeth.

10

as if the one weather is worry
occasional breaks to blue sky
brief sunlight on sodden grass

the lyric will haunt me forever

I prefer not to travel

sitting then at a table
in southwestern France

nor can I stray far from story
overcast   cloud cover   periods of rain
no hope of location

11

pretend you're not alone   imagine
your mother might still be alive
conjure the answer
the light at the end
of a life
let them believe you can sing like Diana Krall
play piano   tap dance   stand on your head
pretend you know
little of death
pretend there's a god
or a goddess   something supreme
pretend
there's someone
in charge
someone who cares

12

do your words translate
undiluted
behind iris and optic nerve
from where into what lingual joy

the wind blows and
masses of blossoms
fall into the street   it gusts and
a wren blows onto your bed

you translate me
into a conscious connection
I comprehend

13

you say the world is all one
you say what happens to me
happens to you

that the world
must rest from its frenzy
its unceasing spin

the same world

I could be your green mountain
or not-so-green mountain
you be my tree

14

The volume of narrative
its wide-reaching long-lasting
exponentiates   explodes

its functions wax
wane
sometimes they blame

right now I have only words on my mind
no story at all
no plotline   tangent   no arc   no she said she said

soft-hearted showers polish the overnight street
a line loops me back

to rest in a small space
a basket of pansies
a bowl of clear water
a box of bright bracing words
three or four unstoried thoughts

15

I take you to bed more than once
lights on
when else can be *Time*

is it a crime to interpret   interpolate
inveigle you
my soul of the world   spun gold
a form of fable

some say you are inimitable
mirror cell mirror cell
on the blank page

who among us
is faultless
faithful   sufficiently sage

> *The distinction between past, present, and future*
> *is only a stubbornly persistent illusion.*
>
> —Einstein

I'm no match for this thrall
sensors all over my body
eyes inside ears

earth worms sport taste buds
all over their pink elasticized skin
a form of ecstatic

if time is a myth
then aging is fantasy

although bodies
these soft unfolding formations
finally prove

each one   our own
unwavering directional dart

17

your poems are footsteps
in sand
tracks
to follow   blameless transitions
slow transformations softly recounting
Paris to a Greek island
a bedroom whitewashed
a vineyard in the green Napa Valley
the mountain you love
veiled in translation   uttered
possibly altered
is this what you mean to say

18

cloud cover protects us from vast cosmic flame
conflagration

endothelial cells
guard us inside our skulls

what guards us from nighttime
from bleak streets   basements
vitriol   bile
from ourselves
from the rile inside the mind

is there ever safety enough

and yet   we are always there
with ourselves
can anyone be
more comprehending

19

the clamour of story
exhausts the worldwide
spacetime
Cosmic Background Noise
incessant
steady-state
this dangerous diet of human
inhuman accounts

hearts   ears   eyes

20

this is the way a legend
the way it is told
the once-upon-a
they said
is how we learn
non-binary notwithstanding
is how we
this story
relearn   unlearn   learn all over again
or so they say   said

21

philosophies embellish her while
languages
languages endow her tongue
she's political but not greedy
during the war she refused to use French

there are sheep in the blue bloated sky
bloated   frothing in
        floating out

a camel never goes dry
a tiger never goes hungry

Paris beds her while Greece
O Greece   the sea there
tenders her crowns of turquoise and gold
sea collars   salted white lace
riffled foam at slack tide

which home is home

California
is another dimension

22

you say on page 82 that the heart
sets up its own heart equations
I say you are nowhere in sight

concerning time
no one understands
its subsistence

to know so little of interpretation
there were no birds
no murmurations
inside these perfected pages

no roses or grape lilacs   no floribunda at all
no ribbons   neither red ribbons nor blue
only words in their best unlilted order

a place for the genuine
heart to heart
facial detection   some recognition

Pop Culture 1

Why is it so difficult to see the lesbian?... In part because she has been
"ghosted"—or made to seem invisible by culture itself.

—Terry Castle

In the last century the twentieth the late nineteen-nineties everyone wanted
to be a lesbian this may be exaggeration maybe not everyone maybe not
Pope Saint Paul II or John Ashbery or Sarah Palin but many enough lesbians
being the media darlings of that period of time TV magazines photomontages
the lesbian at last at long long last becoming visible transmuting the zeitgeist
a time out of time refreshingly free of sham
if you can't bring back the past
                    in time you can
                            bring forth the future.

23

pursuing this trail
these traces   your perfumed vernaculars
dialects   this dimension of life
concerned mainly with dialogues
of candid connection
a line to
a line from

geometries of unhurried care
lineal arrangements
cornered and squared

this planet   this freaky fragility
this bright blue protection   and porous
a blue line around   stratospheric
thin shield and circled   mindspace and sky

24

the material conditions of this particular bond
is a book
letters and binding and ink

is the fact of
women and
women   sanguine oceanic

is litristic psychic cerebral
diaphanous strands

all attachment is optimistic
says Lauren Berlant

a certain corner on a subconscious street
women and books binding

25

coming to me in the night
nothing is moving   although
there is always street traffic
and the backyard is filled at all times
with small apple trees

in the house a phrase on the move
holding its blent bated breath
and in the dark
a small square of white
waiting

you
mining my mind
as I sleep
this is how it goes   how I compose
I don't really know who you are

26

The presumption of this
as vast as a prairie night sky

from the edge of a wheatfield
pinpricks of entreaty
how many lightyears
of longing

27

in love with their sound
their number   their spacings   their knit
their purling shapes
your words
I see
hear them
inside these compact
these compartments of amplification
how they stream   slip-sliding   their
tensile   their directional
strength   frank and capable sense
their colour is not only music

Pop Culture 2

Why is it so difficult to see the lesbian…
—Terry Castle

A woman who loves a woman is
a dyke yes   is gay they say   an invert   a sapphist
is lesbo   is queer   a friend of Dorothy
a member of the lodge   sings in the choir
        is the "L" in LGBTQ2S+
is invisible
is a small square of lilac
of evidence
a small square of letters
is a comfort   a hand mirror   right-angled
right under
is thunder
a fine-forked resistance   a consistent reassurance
remember the marches
the meetings collective   the premeditated
the deliberate liberation
the swagger of unconventional views
the other side of tradition
is a looking glass   reflecting
upstream
a small square of likeness
reflecting the world

28

is the light at the end
closer in your rear-view
than in mine

maybe your tunnel
one end to the other
has been lit all along

my mother still sits
in dim lamplight
when she knits

the sweaters
are always for somebody else

29

in the Canadian Rockies bears speak
neither English nor French nor Kutenai
nor Arabic   nor will they stay
inside their considerable mountain-side squares

to sight a grizzly
at the far end of a trail
is both bespoke
lucky   and not

the screed granite walls
the brief sunlight there
casting
overlong shadows

language then
is of little assistance
you are forced
to fall back on unfortified faith

thank you   mouthing thank you
and please
addressing the universe
mouthing no thank you too

the common grizzly
can cover vast distances
faster than the word
fear

30

these mountains push out of the earth
as if walls   moss-flocked and soft-treed
as if to create spaces for gods

we who drive by
driving through these peaked granite chambers
are dwarfed
are deified too

31

even death
   you speak of your own
and the planet Mars
you know fear
but so little

I have turned my ankle
I lie in this mountain-lodge bed
imagining a fire at night
incendiary
the pain
is that provocative

because I cannot   will not   write
about the sixth mass extinction
I write instead
about my own death
(not yours)

the fulcrum there
criss-crossing the ice-blue abyss

I am not the only one dying

in a bed
early summer late morning
on rose-scented pillows
bloodless the bedfolds
a fold of rag paper   a pen
sunlight through the wide window
blistering the blue room to white

there are two unblighted pears on a plate
and fourteen blackberries

this may not be true
this may not be me
dying
leaving ink stains and bone

this may become the extinction
leaving
roaches and rats under floorboards and cases of wine

33

Words are the staple we crave
never mind honeyed milk   sweet-buttered bread

so much who we are
is fledged in conversation

conversant with others
shifts who we have been

despite tight shoes and eyeglasses

how would a rose be known
without those four letters to frame it

would a mouth   would eyes
without *eyes*

when we look in
would we know what we see

A Blessing

for Janette and Rachael

This is what a blessing is   forty years   waking up every morning side by side
leaving the house through the front door   enduring so little   a blessing
only a few men in the street who holler which has happened only three times
a blessing   and once two boys spitting close range   saliva running down
the front of her coat   dog shit from a speeding car once   threats of hurt
the nighttime streets empty   how fast we ran

years asking for the common privilege of benefits   workplace
same sex   services denied   we are lesbians   we are small women
and the world does not care if we are friendly or kind   we do not
hold hands in the park   we do not kiss goodbye in the car
we are not what we are supposed to be   but this is Canada
this is what a blessing is   this is not a country where the death penalty
might apply

when men no longer have / power over women, over whom / will they have it?

—Etel Adnan

When women no longer bend
descend blend spend
their days fending
or end their days mending
their feelings or his
pretending
defending
tending
the men

how far then
will be their reach

35

It has been forty years
since we first promised at first to forestall
those three words

those three consequential sequential
words   avoiding jinx
defending ourselves from impulsive cliché

o yes   we were forked-lightning
and thunder   roses climbed wild
round our wrists and our throats   red roses and pink

morning glories and rain
on hot summer days
rainbows and wine

o yes   we had moonless nights
the North Star blessing our heads
we had our whole lithesome bodies

but those three rushing words
one after another
                              we held out forty days
it has been forty years

A Certain Uncertain State of Affairs

after Mark Halliday's "Couples"

*because [the lesbian] has been "ghosted"—or made to seem invisible—
by culture itself.*
—Terry Castle

All the old lesbians in their old import cars.
She's a brunette, the other's a blond.
They do not call themselves old.
The car's a wagon, unwashed,
but as long as it takes them from their house to the movies,
they don't care. Most nights
it's dark and the neighbours
have lives of their own.

They get their hair dyed in another town.

They leave the house in a hurry that night
injuring the brunette's hip, maybe her back
trying to get to the movie on time.

Her sister's a redhead,
also a lesbian.
Last week her sister called to say
she'd grown old overnight.
That happens, but mostly in fiction.
Woke up with runnels, nose to her chins:
marionette lines.

The brunette worries about looking too much
like her mother
who is dead. A cause for worry.

The blond worries about acting too much
like her father
if you know what I mean.
They leave the house in a light rain
to watch *The Reader* at nine,
but remember when they get there that the movie
starts at nine-thirty,
parking lot full, first show still on.
The Reader is a four-star romance: adolescent boy, older woman
blond, not that much older.
They get a lot of that,
these old lesbians: boy/girl/blond,
even though so much has now been reinvented.

They haven't given up on the world
but it's not simple.
Today the cooking spray wouldn't spray, the nozzle jammed up, all skittery.
They took it back.
They still call themselves lesbians.
She subscribes to *Lesbian Connection*.
Pronouns have always been problematic.
The other was a separatist in her mid-twenties.

They sit in the parking lot in the rain.
They're not married. But they could be. Now. That's the law.

They used to be afraid of each other.
Other people, like the neighbours, call them lesbians too,
if they call them anything; old women are always in danger
of disappearing.

After a while the rain picks up. The narrative too.
Twenty-nine years.
The blond has forgotten her Tilley hat.
Maybe they'll get married next week. Maybe
they're more afraid of each other than ever:

they still have their principles.
Maybe they never
were kicked out of paradise.
You'd have to speak to them about that in person.

They don't stay, they don't see the movie.
There's still so much to do, reinvent. It's raining.
They're disappearing.
They don't have time
to sit around in a dark parking lot.

36

Today the wind
blew broken sunshine all over the street
bouncing leaf shadow and shine
palimpsesting the road   racing
bright daytime stars

I want to consume this
untamed incandescence
this radiance   hungry for
illumination
for one single insight
to brighten inside

37

A serene square of fathomless vertical invention
perception
cubing the depth

compared to the clamour of chronicles
who   how   plotlines   protagonists
words   whence and why
       with what
typewriter or kitchen knife
narrative arc   stopwatch

object and action   watcher and watched
eyewitness   beloved   smitten
smite   stalker and stalked

compared to phrase

you don't even know who I am

I am   this mindless supplicant
who pesters your sleep

38

Poetry is philosophy in evening-wear.

—Kevin Heslop

With your words
your philosophical contours and colours
I confess my fixation

with your poetries as blameless
as your truth-seeking self

as selfless
you will soon be one hundred years old

I have fallen in love
with a century   some sort of phase

my wife doesn't mind   she knows
I have fallen in love with an arrant ideal

I have kissed women
I have let women kiss me

and yet I have never seen
Death in Venice

nor have I heard Umm Kulthum sing
her astonishing songs

neither have I walked the slopes of Mt. Tamalpais
in the red light of morning

I would like to paint squares of abstraction
I would like to arrive in a boat

I admire their stride   the women   the ingenuity
of their impossible lives   the way we continue to thrive

you say love is the most
is the foremost existential we face

I too ask questions   I value words
if you were a flower   you would be a bird

Paris   I would like to speak French   I would like
to abide
for a time
in the city of lights

everything about you makes sense

Time is what the clock says.

—Einstein

One day the woman's watch slowed
losing at first only five seconds
five minutes
later ten maybe twelve

over days the silver wristwatch
with its moon face its white face
reliably slowed
slowly
so that the time it proposed
could no longer
be trusted

so few wear a wristwatch these days
the passage of time beginning to stumble
as if time itself might decide
to disappear

still we check:
cell phone   coffee break   lunch

the battery of course was replaced
at midnight the two silver hands
rejoined conjointly
reaching up once again in timed supplication

in the same way the sun continues to set   moon to rise
despite Copernicus   despite even Einstein
we treat these misconceptions
as if they are real

41

We are in Syria
in the dream in a Syrian town
you are as you are
a Syrian poet
Maureen in support
ties a red ribbon to the rails of a chair

it's true
I've been watching too much TV
red ribbons red roses pose too many risks
in my sleep not knowing
the Algerian war   the two
or three brutal sides

you stopped writing in French
                              started painting instead

it's true
a dream is always a poem
while a poem is not always a dream

roses are not always painted in sanguineous French

In the 4 a.m.

For my wife

the chorusing rain so ravishing
we rush out of the house to make love
a before-dawn silvery love
the cupped radiance
streetlights bright as up-swelling joy

the rain so glamorous we light up two cigarettes
our backs puddled in boulevard grass
under bare trees we study the miniature
tear-drop chandeliers   blow collapsible smoke
into felled funnels of wet

the rain so clamorous
our breathing slows as though
we've started to live underground

in Montreal I wanted to make love on Mount Royal
wintertime   especially in winter   to climb the low slope
blankets in sacks for the snow
to press small warming dents under the boughs
my husband at the time declining the white invitation
though I asked more than once

but tonight   this soft fizzley falling
this rain insistent as pins
the contact so unmistakable
murmurous   cool   the undertones
the universe falling
again and again

42

weak-kneed in the presence of beauty
in the thrall of her eloquent words

this deluge of yearning
which is to say

be wary

this seduction of language
metaphor
the elision of disparate matters
the thrill of rhythm   rhyme
timing
the refrain of verbal persuasion

which is to say
poetry must always be tested
for truth

43

Two women make love
on top of Mount Maxwell   mid-afternoon
later
three motorcycles arrive at the peak

timing

once
the two women made love
in a theatre downtown   early show
they no longer recall the show's name

delight is encountered   did you say
not only in bedrooms

44

at sea level time lazes about
                        at the beach
St. Tropez or perhaps Cote d'Azur
where a minute can last
a whole afternoon

short lines
slow
the pace
of a poem

on the top of a mountain Mount Sannine or Tamalpais near Sausalito
time flies

a life unimpeded is a wink is a blink of an eye

the eye
is always your own

45

my life has not been riddled with bullets
nor has my house been burned to the ground
I have never been raped or beaten or thrown down
a set of back stairs
or drowned
nor does Death hang from the trees
where I live

nevertheless my head bears these facts
my mind contains reports on the 8 a.m. news
shootings   Miami   Kabul   a school in the suburbs
a knifing downtown

my mind doesn't stop at the edges of me

the world is a staggering place
the mind is a staggering world

46

this is merely a record
a reflective long-distance affection
a crazy cacophonous crush
traces of memory   traces of mind
a missive
a meditation
geometries   paginations   new ways of placing

California is a long way by foot
a short way by word
a state
a space in what we call time

Paris is farther

you say love
is the only salvation you know

47

parts of me are falling back into history
fading
backward into the once-upon

irrelevance is not a complaint
I know
a slender blue ribbon rivers my life
this is a recognition   a far-flung regard

there are still rivers   there are lakes of green water
the word love twins the word kind

the twentieth-first century tapers
now into reckoning   reconcile

I try to live in the present
but the present is blindingly short-lived

therefore   sotto voce   into the future   infinity
nothing there is guaranteed
this is just how it is

48

later you will write about silence
trying
to invoke quietude
in this noisome place

conjuring a place of no sound
you are a poet writing backwards
purging words
trying to cultivate wordlessness
invoking eternity   that worrisome place
as if you are writing your own death
testing the possibilities of
what we call real

as if you could paint with sea mist or raindrops
or tears

when the noise becomes deafening
silence prevails

49

words are
together they
brumble   oceanic
the ear too
is a shell is
waves are
trees too are waving
any tree with or without pinnated leaves
or live needles
and a river of course a river
a mountain even a hill a small hill
a slice of same sunlight   crisp
adjacent a charcoal blue shadow
words are
I am
you are
already perfect
already a poem

1. I am grateful for the poetry of Adèle Barclay, Adrienne Rich, Alexa De Weil, Alice Bloch, Alison Colbert, Alix Dobkin, Ana Kowalkowska, Anne Cameron, Annick MacAskill, Audrey Lorde, Barbara Noda, Barbara Smith, Becky Birtha, Betsy Warland, Bobbie Bishop, C. Allyson Lee, Candis Graham, Carol Camper, Carolina Pasqueira, Caroline Duffy, Carolyn Gammon, Cherríe Moraga, Cheryl Clark, Christina Springer, Christine Donald, Chrystos, Clare Coss, Connie Fife, Daphne Marlatt, Dionne Brand, Djuna Barnes, Doris L. Harris, Donayle l. Hammond, Donna Allega, Dorothy Allison, Eaton Hamilton, Eileen Myles, Elana Dykewomon, Elise Young, Elizabeth Bishop, Elizabeth Phillips, Ellen Bass, Ellen Marie Bissert, Elsa Gidlow, Eleanor Lerman, Emily Dickinson, Erín Moure, Esther Silverman, Etel Adnan, Felice Newman, Florence Wyle, Fran Winant, Frankie Hucklenbroich, Gertrude Stein, Gloria Anzaldúa, Helen Humphreys, Hiromi Goto, Honor Moore, Indigo Som, Irene Klepfisz, Jacqueline Lapidus, Jaisne Blue Sexton, Jan Clausen, Jane Byers, Jane Creighton, Jean Mollison, Joan Larkin, Judith Castle, Judith McDaniel, Judith Nicholson, Judy Grahn, Julie Blackwomon, June Jordan, Karen Brodine, Karla E. Rosales, Kay Ryan, Kayla Czaga, Karen Miranda Augustine, Kit Yee Chan, Kitty Tsui, Lanuola Asiasiga, Leleta Kamu, Leah Horlick, Lorraine Sutton, Lynn Strongin, Lydia Kwa, M.F. Hershman, Marguerite Yourcenar, Maria Amparo Jimenez, Maria Cora, Marilyn Hacker, Martha Courtot, Martha Shelley, Mary Oliver, May Sarton, May Swenson, Maureen Hynes, Marg Yeo, Marianne Moore and Mary Anne Moore, Melanie Kaye, Michele Chai, Michelle Cliff, Milagros Paredes, Minnie Bruce Pratt, Natalie Diaz, Nicole Brossard, Noriko Oka, Olga Broumas, Osa Hidalgo de la Riva, Pat Parker, Rebecca Gordon, Renée Vivien, Rita Mae Brown, Ritz Chow, Robin Becker, Romaine Brooks, Rota Silvestrini, Ruthe D. Canter, Sabrina D. Hernandez, SDiane A. Bogus, Sappho, Sapphire, Shani Mootoo, Sharon Barba, Shenaz L. Stri, Skye Ward, Susan Beaver, Susan Griffin, Susan Saxe, Tina Biello, Victoria Lena Manyarrows, Wendy Brooks Wieber, Wendy Donawa, Wendt Stevens, Willyce Kim, Wilmette Brown, and many, many others for their presence, their keening, their inspiration, courage and spirit, which hold me up, sustain me.

2. Several lines in this collection make reference to lines in poems in Etel Adnan's *Time*: i) on page 11, "voyage of no return" refers to the same phrase on page 76 in *Time*; ii) the phrase "at the edge of evil and good," also on page 11, refers to a similar phrase on page 87 in *Time*; iii) "nor does Death hang from the trees" on page 61 appears in *Time* (slightly altered) on page 57; iv) the phrase "riddled with bullets" on page 61 has been borrowed from the poem on page 30 in *Time*.

3. On page 11, to die "full of days" refers to the Bible, Job: 42:17: "And Job died, an old man, and full of days."

4. On page 20, "it gusts and / a wren blows onto your bed" is borrowed, slightly altered, from a Facebook post by Johnny Aiken.

5. On page 30, the phrase "a place for the genuine" is taken from the poem "Poetry" by Marianne Moore.

6. On page 37, the poem *Pop Culture 2* uses some terms found in Alix Dobkin's song "Lesbian Code."

7. On page 57, "In the 4 a.m." © 2020 by Arleen Paré, *Earle Street*, Vancouver, BC, is reprinted with permission from Talonbooks.

8. Much gratitude to Maureen Hynes, who recommended Etel Adnan's poetry to me.

9. So many many thanks to my wife, Chris Fox, first reader and in-house editor par excellence.

10. And finally, it is with enormous humility and gratitude to Etel Adnan for her celestial poetry and its inspiration, without which I would not have been able to write this collection.

About the Author

Arleen Paré is the author of seven collections of poetry, including *Paper Trail* (NeWest Press, 2007), *Lake of Two Mountains* (Brick Books, 2014), *He Leaves His Face in the Funeral Car* (Caitlin Press, 2015), and *First* (Brick Books, 2021). Her work has been short-listed for the Dorothy Livesay Poetry Prize and has won the American Golden Crown Award for Poetry, the City of Victoria Butler Book Prize, a CBC Bookie Award, and a Governor Generals' Award for Poetry. She lives in Victoria, BC, with her wife, Chris Fox.

AUTHOR PHOTO BY CHRIS FOX.